READING SUCCESS FOR
MINECRAFTERS

Grades 3-4

Illustrated by Amanda Brack

Sky Pony Press
New York

D1451242

Copyright © 2017 by Hollan Publishing, Inc.

Minecraft® is a registered trademark of Notch Development AB.

The Minecraft game is copyright © Mojang AB.

Sky Pony Press books may be purchased in bulk at special discounts for sales promotion, corporate gifts, fund-raising, or educational purposes. Special editions can also be created to specifications. For details, contact the Special Sales Department, Sky Pony Press, 307 West 36th Street, 11th Floor, New York, NY 10018 or info@skyhorsepublishing.com.

Sky Pony® is a registered trademark of Skyhorse Publishing, Inc.®, a Delaware corporation.

Visit our website at www.skyponypress.com.

Authors, books, and more at SkyPonyPressBlog.com.

10 9 8 7 6 5 4

Library of Congress Cataloging-in-Publication Data is available on file.

Cover design by Brian Peterson

Cover illustration by Amanda Brack

Book design by Kevin Baier

Print ISBN: 978-1-5107-3089-2

Printed in China

A NOTE TO PARENTS

When you want to reinforce classroom skills at home, it's crucial to have kid-friendly learning materials. This *Reading Success for Minecrafters* workbook transforms reading practice into an irresistible adventure complete with diamond swords, zombies, skeletons, and creepers. That means less arguing over homework and more fun overall.

Reading Success for Minecrafters is also fully aligned with National Common Core Standards for 3rd and 4th grade English Language Arts (ELA). What does that mean, exactly? All of the reading exercises in this book correspond to what your child is expected to learn in school. This eliminates confusion and builds confidence for greater homework-time success!

As the workbook progresses, the reading becomes more advanced. Encourage your child to progress at his or her own pace. Learning is best when students are challenged, but not frustrated. What's most important is that your Minecrafter is engaged in his or her own learning.

Whether it's the joy of seeing their favorite game characters on every page or the thrill of discovering new words, there is something in this workbook to entice even the most reluctant reader.

Happy adventuring!

PREFIXES

A prefix comes at the beginning of a complete word and turns it into a new word.

un   re   de   under   over   out

1. *Fill in the blank spaces with the new word.*

un + pack = _____   under + take = _____

de + fuse = _____   over + do = _____

re + read = _____   out + live = _____

2. *Choose the correct word to complete the sentences below.*

A. The program shut down and now I have to _____ it.
[remake / reopen]

B. I made a mistake building my tower, so I think I'll _____ it.
[undo / defrost]

C. After I'm done using a pressure plate, I can _____ it.
[deactivate / refinish]

D. The creeper headed toward me but I _____ it.
[underbid / outran]

SUFFIXES

A suffix comes at the end of a word. These suffixes help you make comparisons. When a root word ends in *y*, the *y* changes to an *i* when a suffix is added.

er   **est**   **ier**   **iest**

1.   *Number the words in each column below in the order of least to most.*

_____ loud   _____ funnier

_____ loudest   _____ funny

_____ louder   _____ funniest

2.   *Fill in the blank spaces below.*

smart + _____ = smarter

hard + _er_ = _____

cool + _____ = coolest

happy + _er_ = _____

sunny + _____ = sunniest

long + _est_ = _____

3

PREFIXES

A prefix comes at the beginning of a complete word and turns it into a new word.

1. *Use the prefixes below to complete the sentences.*

mis   ir   dis   co

A. Susan _____ liked playing in Creative mode.

B. Jack _____ judged the location of his first shelter.

C. The kids would have to _____ operate to gather all the resources they needed.

D. It was _____ responsible of that griefer to steal their best items.

E. Their parents would _____ approve if they knew the kids had gone over their screen time limits.

F. Jack and Susan _____ agreed about whether they should trade the emeralds to a villager.

2. *Use each of the prefixes and one of the nouns to create four new words.*

Prefixes	mis	ir	dis	re

Nouns	cover	regular	place
	rational	appear	trust

_____   _____

_____   _____

SUFFIXES

A suffix comes at the end of a complete word and turns it into a new word.

1. *Use the suffixes below to complete the sentences.*

ful   less   ness   ment

A. Steve was brave and fear_____ as he battled the Ender Dragon.

B. When Alex opened the chest, she was blinded by the bright_____ of the diamonds.

C. Steve explored the base_____ of the villager's house.

D. Alex felt help_____ when she was outnumbered by a group of skeletons.

E. She stared at the giant zombie in amaze_____.

F. He used a potion of Weak_____ on the cave spider to reduce its strength.

2. *Use each of the suffixes and one of the nouns to create four new words.*

Suffixes	*ful*	*less*	*ness*	*ment*
Nouns	hope	base	light	care
	sad	dark	home	enjoy

_____   _____

_____   _____

VOWEL-CONSONANT-E SPELLING PATTERN

When a word or the final syllable of a word ends in *e*, then the first vowel is usually long and the *e* is silent.

Examples:

tap + e = tape   mop + e = mope

bit + e = bite   cub + e = cube

1. *Circle the words that fit the vowel-consonant-e pattern.*

chase	smelt	make	brew
teleport	slime	cake	cast
blaze	plank	steep	tame

2. *Write four new words that fit the vowel-consonant-e pattern.*

_____   _____

_____   _____

SUFFIX -ING SPELLING PATTERN

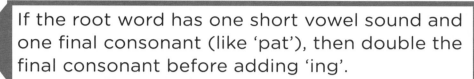

If the root word has one short vowel sound and one final consonant (like 'pat'), then double the final consonant before adding 'ing'.

pat + ing = patting   chop + ing = chopping

let + ing = letting   run + ing = running

sit + ing = sitting

1.  *Spell the following words using the -ing suffix.*

A. cut + ing = _____   **B.** dig + ing = _____

C. fan + ing = _____   **D.** bed + ing = _____

E. stop + ing = _____   **F.** plan + ing = _____

G. stun + ing = _____   **H.** trip + ing = _____

2. *Fill out the chart, writing the original word before the suffix -ing was added.*

ORIGINAL WORD	-ing	Final word
	-ing	winning
	-ing	mapping
	-ing	getting
	-ing	wagging

PLURAL NOUN SPELLING PATTERNS

When a noun ends in ss, sh, ch, or x, add es to make it plural.

Examples:

grass + es = grasses

fish + es = fishes

rich = es = riches

1.

A. box= _____

B. kiss= _____

C. match = _____

D. bush = _____

E. mix = _____

F. witch = _____

G. crash = _____

H. lunch = _____

2.

ORIGINAL WORD	-es	Final word
	-es	sandwiches
	-es	wishes
	-es	catches
	-es	hoaxes

HOMOPHONES

> **Remember:** *Homophones* are words that sound the same but have different meanings.

1. *Use the words from the box to complete each sentence.*

their	they're	there

A. The kids are playing in _____ school's playground.

B. In a few minutes, _____ going to play a game of tag.

C. The school is over _____.

2. *Use the words from the box to complete each sentence.*

too	to	two

A. Cassie drew _____ clouds.

B. Enrico wants _____ go home soon.

C. "I want to play _____," said James.

3. *Select the correct word to complete each sentence.*

A. "What are you drawing over _____?" Dennis asked.
[here / hear]

B. "What? I didn't _____you," Cassie said. **[here / hear]**

C. "Is that _____ basketball?" Penny asked. **[your / you're]**

D. "_____ going to be late getting home," Enrico warned.
[your / you're]

SYNONYMS

Remember: Two words that have the same meaning are *synonyms*.

The Zombie Trap
Read the passage about zombies.

Zombies are so slow and lumbering that it is easy to escape them. Their low, groaning sounds alert you that they are nearby. Another way to <u>elude</u> a zombie is to stay in the sun. Zombies prefer the shade because sunlight will <u>obliterate</u> them in a matter of seconds. Zombies can <u>summon</u> other zombies to <u>expedite</u> an attack on their enemies. If a zombie attacks you, it can <u>transform</u> you into a zombie too.

1. *Write the <u>underlined</u> word from the passage that is the same as each definition below.*

    A. Turn into = _____   **B.** Destroy = _____

    C. Get away from = _____   **D.** Speed up = _____

    E. Call, gather = _____

2. *Find a word in the passage that is a synonym for the words below.*

    A. Warn, signal = _____   **B.** Harm, strike = _____

    C. Foes, rivals = _____

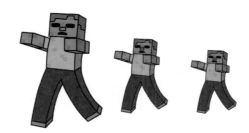

ANTONYMS

> **Remember:** Two words that have opposite meanings are *antonyms*.

3. *Write the <u>underlined</u> word from the passage that is the opposite of each definition below.*

A. Make better = _____

B. Keep the same = _____

C. Send away = _____

D. Catch, tackle = _____

E. Slow down = _____

4. *Find a word in the passage that is an antonym for the words below.*

A. Capture, find = _____

B. Distant, far away = _____

C. Quick, speedy = _____

SYNONYMS

Remember: Two words that have the same meaning are *synonyms*.

Creepers Really Creep Me Out

Read the passage about creepers.

A **horde** of creepers can be **exceptionally** quiet, so you need to be alert at all times. Creepers will sneak up on you and then **detonate** themselves. This will **demolish** anything near the blast. However, there is an easy way to protect yourself. Creepers are **petrified** of cats, so keep a cat with you at all times. Creepers also like to hide in caves, so beware any dark, hidden areas where one could be lurking.

1. Match each **bold** word from the passage to its synonym.

Horde	**Explode**
Exceptionally	**Scared**
Detonate	**Mob**
Demolish	**Very**
Petrified	**Ruin**

2. Find a word in the passage that is a synonym *for the words below.*

A. _____ Explosion, boom

B. _____ Defend, shield

C. _____ Concealed, unseen

ANTONYMS

> **Remember:** Two words that have opposite meanings are *antonyms*.

3. *Select the* antonym *from the list of words and write it on the line next to the* **bold** *word from the passage.*

implode	few	lots	slightly	fix
fearless	extremely	destroy	scared	explode

Horde   _____

Exceptionally   _____

Detonate   _____

Demolish   _____

Petrified   _____

4. *Find a word in the passage that is an antonym for the words below.*

A. _____ Hard, difficult

B. _____ Loud, noisy

C. _____ Bright, sunny

VOCABULARY DEVELOPMENT

Read the passage about the Ender Dragon.

The Ender Dragon

The Ender Dragon <u>appears</u> in each world's End. Black with <u>glowing</u> violet eyes, she spits Ender acid from her mouth. The Ender Dragon circles in the air until she swoops down at a player, <u>charging</u> for the player's lower waist. In the process, she destroys any blocks she passes through, except for obsidian, bedrock, iron bars, and End stone. When a player kills an Ender Dragon, she drops experience orbs, <u>activates</u> the exit portal, and <u>spawns</u> a dragon egg on top of the portal. The exit portal leads to the Outer End.

1. *Match the underlined word from the story to a word in the box that has a* similar *meaning.*

shining	stops	arrives	reproduces
triggers	rushing	divides	

Appears _____   Spawns _____

Charging _____   Glowing _____

Activates _____

2. *Find a word in the passage that is* similar *to the words below.*

A. Doorway, entrance _____

B. Dives, plunges _____

C. Destroys, exterminates _____

VOCABULARY DEVELOPMENT

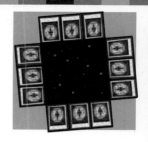

3. Connect the underlined word from the story to the word that has the opposite meaning.

Appears	Retreating
Charging	Vanishes
Activates	Dim
Spawns	Disables
Glowing	Destroys

4. Find a word in the passage that is different *from the words below.*

A. Upper, topmost   _____

B. Swallows, sips   _____

C. Picks up   _____

DEFINING WORDS BY CONTEXT

Remember: *Context* means the text surrounding a word. If you don't know a word, you can sometimes figure out what it means by the words around it.

Read the passage about gardening. Then choose a word from the passage that matches each definition.

Gardening

Steve will need plenty of food. The best way to get sustenance is to grow a garden of fresh vegetables. First he will need to assemble a wooden hoe to dig the garden. This hoe requires two sticks and two pieces of lumber as well as a crafting table. He will also need seeds for the types of vegetables he wants to plant. Finally, he will need a bucket to hold water and a torch to put next to his crops to provide light.

When Steve has his inventory together, it is time to till the soil. He clears a piece of land to make it level. Then he puts the hoe in the ground and drags it toward him, turning over a couple of inches of soil. He makes evenly spaced furrows to hold the seeds, allowing enough room for the plants to spread out. Steve distributes the seeds evenly in the rows, and then covers them lightly with soil.

Next, it's time to excavate a hole in the ground for water. Steve transfers water into the hole with his bucket. Then he puts the torch next to his crops to impart light. The torch will also deter monsters from consuming his plants.

1. _____ food

2. _____ to make or put something together

3. _____ a piece of wood

4. _____ a collection of supplies

16

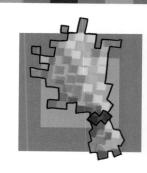

1. *Circle the letter that is the best description for the word from the passage.*

Require
   a. give   **b.** take   **c.** need

Provide
   a. take away   **b.** offer   **c.** shine

Till
   a. plow   **b.** plant   **c.** water

Distribute
   a. give out   **b.** hold   **c.** gather

Excavate
   a. create   **b.** dig   **c.** cover

Impart
   a. hide   **b.** give off   **c.** brighten

Deter
   a. prevent   **b.** invite   **c.** scare

2. *Read the sentences from the passage. Then circle the word in blue that means the same thing as the word in bold.*

A. He clears a piece of land to make it **level**. [flat / at an angle]

B. Steve **transfers** water into the hole with his bucket.
    [drizzles / moves]

C. The torch will also deter monsters from **consuming** his plants.
    [digging up / eating]

17

DEFINING WORDS BY CONTEXT

Read the passage about diamond armor. Then choose a word from the passage to complete the definitions.

Diamond Armor

Diamond armor is the strongest covering for a Minecrafter. This durable armor protects a player from many types of damage. It will shield you from fire, arrows, lava, cacti, lightning, and explosions. However, it will not shield you from suffocation if you are stuck inside a block or starvation if you run out of food.

You will need 24 diamond units to craft a full set of armor. You will need 5 diamonds to make a helmet and 8 diamonds to make a chestplate. To make leggings you will need 7 diamonds. Boots are made with 4 diamonds. Armor can be enchanted to provide even more protection.

Diamonds are most common in layers five through twelve. Look for their glint in lava lakes and water streams. You will need an iron pickaxe to mine for diamonds.

1. _____ very strong

2. _____ harm, injury

3. _____ having no food to eat

4. _____ having no air to breathe

DEFINING WORDS BY CONTEXT

1. *Complete the chart using words from the passage.*

Word	Definition
	make, create
	protect, defend
	given a charm
	shine, sparkle
	dig up
	protective covering
	blast, burst

2. *Write your own definitions for the words below.*

A. Chestplate: _____

_____

B. Common: _____

_____

MAIN IDEA AND DETAILS

Remember: The *main idea* is what the passage is about. The *details* support the main idea.

Read about igloos. Then answer the questions below.

Igloos

Igloos make a great pit stop if you are traveling. You will find them in cold, snowy biomes, such as the Ice Plains and Cold Taiga. If you get cold or hungry, you might be able to find an empty igloo to hang out in for a while. Inside will be a cozy room with everything you need. It will have a rug, a crafting table, a torch, and a heater. It will have lots of food stored on a shelf. You will also find blankets and warm clothes. Just watch out for polar bears!

1. What is the main idea of this text?

_____

_____

_____

2. List three details that support the main idea.

A. _____

B. _____

C. _____

MAIN IDEA AND DETAILS

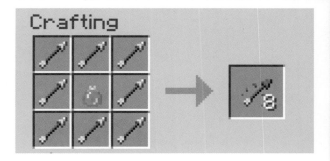

Read about tipped arrows. Then answer the questions below.

Tipped Arrows

Tipped arrows are arrows drenched with one of the potions. They'll give your victim the potion's effect, but only up to one-eighth of the time the original potion lasted. Here's the catch: the potion you use to create a tipped arrow has to be a lingering potion. A lingering potion is any splash potion that has been brewed with a bottle of dragon's breath. And to get the dragon's breath, well, you have to fight the Ender Dragon. And fighting the Ender Dragon is not easy!

1. The main idea of this text is:

   A. Tipped arrows are easy to make.
   B. Tipped arrows have no effect.
   C. Tipped arrows are hard to make.

2. One detail that supports the main idea is:

   A. You need a lingering potion to make a tipped arrow.
   B. Tipped arrows last only one-eighth of the time as the original potion.
   C. Tipped arrows are drenched in a potion.

3. Another detail that supports the main idea is:

   A. You need dragon's breath to make a lingering potion.
   B. Tipped arrows give your victim the potion's effect.
   C. Tipped arrows are the best way to defeat the enemy.

4. Another detail that supports the main idea is:

   A. A lingering potion is made from an original potion.
   B. You'll need to fight an Ender Dragon to get dragon's breath.
   C. Ender Dragons are easy to fight.

COMPARE AND CONTRAST

> **Remember:** When you *compare* two things, you are finding ways they are similar. When you *contrast* two things, you are finding ways they are different.

Read about skeletons and zombies. Then answer the questions.

Skeletons and Zombies

Skeletons like to travel in mobs. They will burn in sunlight, so they try to stay in the shade as much as possible. However, a skeleton will be protected from the sun if it is wearing a helmet. Skeletons drop bones and arrows. They are unable to see through glass. Skeletons are one of the harder mobs to defeat. A single skeleton can spawn almost anywhere in the Overworld at a light level of 7 or less.

Zombies are often found in mobs. Sunlight can kill a zombie but a helmet will protect it. Zombies drop rotten flesh, carrots, and potatoes. They move very slowly, so it is easy to defeat them. Zombies cannot see through glass. In the Overworld, zombies spawn in groups of four.

1. Compare

List three things that skeletons and zombies have in common.

1. _____

2. _____

3. _____

2. Contrast

List three ways that skeletons and zombies are different.

1. _____

2. _____

3. _____

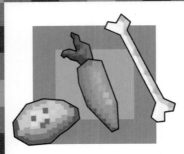

VENN DIAGRAM

Use your lists to fill in the Venn diagram to compare and contrast the traits of skeletons and zombies.

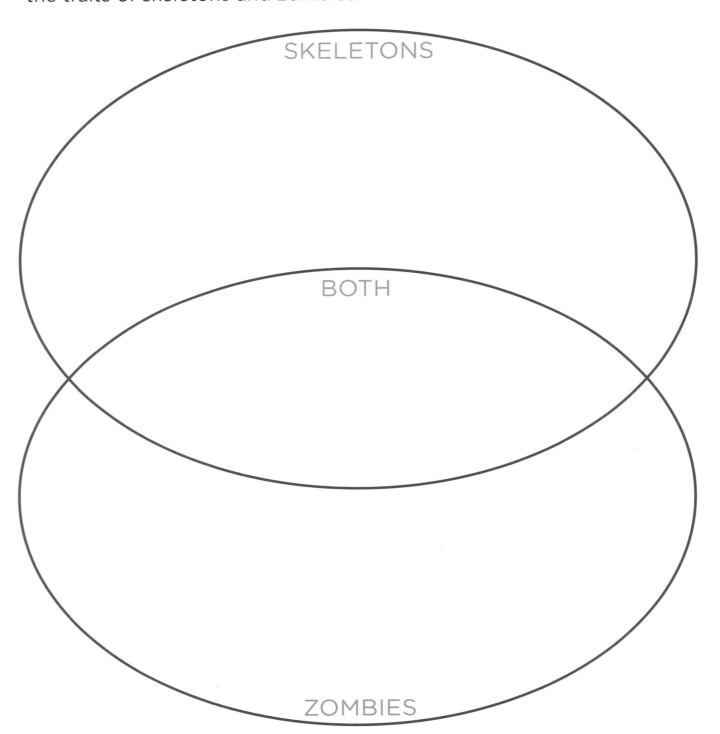

SKELETONS

BOTH

ZOMBIES

POTIONS

Read about potions. Then fill out the chart.

Potions

Potions give you special powers. To make potions, you must collect certain items from the Nether. You also need to have a brewing stand. Almost all potions start with a base potion. When you add a particular ingredient to the base potion, you get a particular effect.

Glistering melon gives you instant health. Its icon is a slice of watermelon. Pufferfish lets you breathe underwater. Its icon is a pufferfish. A spider eye makes the potion poisonous. Its icon is a red spider eye. Sugar gives you speed. Its icon is a sugar crystal. A golden carrot gives you night vision. Its icon is a yellow carrot. A ghast tear, which has the icon of a teardrop, gives you regeneration. You get strength from blaze powder. This icon looks like a small fire.

Ingredient	Icon
Glistering melon	
	Pufferfish
Spider eye	
	Sugar crystal
Golden carrot	
Ghast tear	
	Fire

CAUSE AND EFFECT

Each ingredient in a potion causes *an effect. Using the passage, match the cause with its effect by writing the correct letter on the line.*

Cause	Effect
_____ Glistering melon	**A.** Speed
_____ Pufferfish	**B.** Night vision
_____ Spider eye	**C.** Strength
_____ Sugar	**D.** Poisonous
_____ Golden carrot	**E.** Instant health
_____ Ghast tear	**F.** Breathe underwater
_____ Blaze powder	**G.** Regeneration

ORDER OF EVENTS: GOING FISHING

Read the story about Will and Mina going fishing. Then on the next page number the events in the story in the order in which they happened.

Will stared at the bobber, hoping it would dip into the water. And then it did! He yanked back on the pole and started reeling in his catch.

It was big. It was heavy. It was round and yellow. It was . . . a pufferfish.

"No!" said Will. "Are you kidding me?"

As he unhooked the fish from his line, he heard Mina laughing from behind.

"Hey, you caught a big one!" she teased.

Will shot her a dirty look. "Maybe your bad luck with the cat is rubbing off on me. Did you catch him yet?"

Mina shook her head. "But he'll be back," she said with a smile. "Till then, I'll hang out with you."

Great, thought Will. He was about to toss the pufferfish back into the water when Mina held out her hand.

"Wait!" she said. "I can use that fish to make a potion—the potion of water breathing. My bottle is almost empty."

Will shrugged. "Be my guest," he said, tossing her the fish. Then he cast his line again into the water, hoping for better luck.

The bobber ducked underwater instantly. "Already?" said Will, gripping his pole. "Please don't be a pufferfish. Please don't be a pufferfish," he chanted as he reeled in the line.

As the fish broke the surface of the water, he breathed a sigh of relief. It was a beautiful pink salmon. He could almost taste it now! But as he unhooked the fish, Will had an uneasy feeling—like he was being watched.

From <u>Lost in the Jungle: Secrets of an Overworld Survivor</u>, Book 1 by Greyson Mann, Sky Pony Press, 2017.

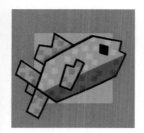

ORDER OF EVENTS GOING FISHING

Number the events in the story in the order in which they happened.

_____ Will hopes he doesn't catch a pufferfish.

_____ Mina teases Will.

_____ Will gives Mina the fish.

_____ Will blames Mina for his bad luck.

_____ Mina holds out her hand for the fish.

_____ Will unhooks the salmon.

_____ Will casts his fishing line.

_____ Will reels in a salmon.

_____ Will feels uneasy.

_____ Will reels in a pufferfish.

ORDER OF EVENTS: WILL & THE PIG

Read the story about Will and the pig. Then on the next page number the events in the story in the order in which they happened.

This is it, thought Will. It's now or never. He leaned over the fence to scratch the pig's head, and then he reached for the saddle.

Oops! He'd almost forgotten the bait! "Wait here," he said to the pig. "I'll be right back."

Will grabbed his fishing pole and hurried to the garden to find a ripe carrot. As he tugged the leafy green end of one from the dirt, the pig grunted.

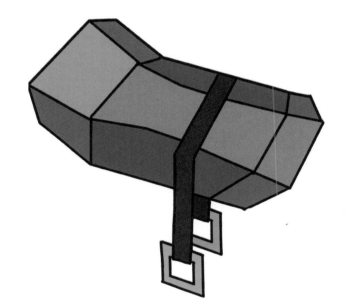

"Easy, boy," said Will, pressing his fishhook through the carrot. "You can eat it, but not quite yet." Then he hurried back to the pigpen and leaned the fishing pole against the fence. The carrot dangled just out of the pig's reach.

As Will placed his saddle gently on the pig's back, the pig grunted a protest. But he kept his black eyes on the carrot.

Will eased himself over the fence and lowered himself onto the saddle. Then he reached for the fishing pole.

"Okay, boy," he said. "Here we go. Follow the carrot!"

Will held the carrot just in front of the pig's nose, leading him left and right around the pen. The pig moved slowly at first and then began to trot. Will held on tight, laughing out loud. It was working. He was actually riding a pig!

From Lost in the Jungle: Secrets of an Overworld Survivor, Book 1 by Greyson Mann, Sky Pony Press, 2017.

ORDER OF EVENTS: WILL & THE PIG

Number the events in the story in the order in which they happened.

_____ Will puts the saddle on the pig.

_____ Will digs up a carrot.

_____ Will grabs his fishing pole.

_____ Will puts the carrot on the fishhook.

_____ Will gets into the saddle.

_____ The pig begins to trot.

_____ Will hurries back to the pigpen.

_____ Will holds the carrot in front of the pig's nose.

WHO, WHAT, WHEN, WHERE, WHY, HOW

Read the story about Lucy and Eric battling the skeletons. Then answer the questions.

"I need a sword!" Lucy cried out, looking frantically at the skeletons.

Eric crouched on the ground in the forest. The sun had set a long time ago, and it was hard to see. He felt through his inventory and found his spare sword. It wasn't ideal, but at least he could give something to Lucy. He hoped it would do. He handed it to Lucy.

"I'm sorry, but I only have a wooden sword."

"That's better than nothing! Thanks!"

Eric started to battle the skeletons with his powerful diamond sword, which he always fought with. He sprinted toward the two skeletons that Lucy had cornered. With a blow from his diamond sword, he defeated one of them. Lucy battled the other one with her wooden sword until it was destroyed.

"We make a great team," Eric said with a smile.

"The fight's not over yet," Lucy said as six new skeletons suddenly appeared and shot arrows at them. Eric's response was cut off as an arrow pierced his leg.

Lucy ran over to her friend and splashed a potion of Invisibility on him. Now the skeletons wouldn't be able to shoot more arrows at Eric.

"We need to find the spawner before it makes more skeletons. Let's go!"

Adapted from Skeleton Battle: The Unofficial Minecrafters Academy Series, Book 2, Sky Pony Press, 2016

1. Draw arrows pointing to the words in the passage that answer this question: **Who are the main characters in the story?**

2. Draw a triangle around the words in the passage that answer this question: **What are the main characters battling?**

3. Underline the words in the passage that give a clue to the answer to this question: **What time of day does this story take place?**

4. Draw a circle around the word in the passage that answers this question: **Where does the arrow pierce Eric?**

5. Draw a wavy line underneath the words in the passage that answer this question: **Why does Lucy say, "The fight's not over yet"?**

6. Draw a rectangle around the words in the passage that answer this question: **How are the skeletons multiplying?**

WHO, WHAT, WHEN, WHERE, WHY, HOW

Use full sentences to answer the following questions about the passage.

1. *Who* are the main characters in the story? _____

_____

_____

2. *What* are the main characters battling?_____

_____

_____

3. *What time of day* does this story take place?_____

_____

_____

4. *Where* does the arrow pierce Eric? _____

_____

_____

5. *Why* does Lucy say, "The fight's not over yet"?_____

_____

_____

6. *How* are the skeletons multiplying? _____

_____

_____

MAKING INFERENCES

Remember: *Inference* is using facts, observations, and logic to come to an assumption or a conclusion. It is not stating what is obvious, or what has clearly been said. Using clues in the text, ask yourself: "What conclusions can I draw about an event or a character?"

Abby's Workshop

Abby loves to make things in her workshop. She has many tools hanging neatly on the wall, including a saw, hammer, and pliers. She keeps a box on the desk to hold small items, such as nails and screws. This makes it easy to find what she needs.

She has another box high up on a shelf. This box is for items that she doesn't need all the time. Plus, some of the things in the box can be harmful if swallowed, such as glue. She keeps them up high so her dog will not get into them. Her dog, Tootsie, is curious about everything and often gets into trouble. She will lick or eat just about anything!

The lamp on the desk is for when Abby works on small projects. The lamp helps her see details better, and it keeps her from squinting. She also needs good light so she can sweep up sawdust at the end of the day.

Abby's stool is always tucked under the desk when she isn't using it. She doesn't want her baby brother to trip over it. Sometimes she babysits him when her mom and dad are busy. She likes to take him into her workshop and show him what she is making. She hopes when he gets older he'll want to learn how to make things too. Then she will teach him how to use the tools and they will make things together. As long as he keeps her workshop just the way she likes it!

MAKING INFERENCES

For every inference you make, give three clues from the text.

1. What can you infer about Abby's character traits? _____

_____

_____

2. What are three clues in the text that helped you draw this inference?

_____

_____

3. What can you infer about the types of projects Abby makes?

_____

_____

4. What are three clues in the text that helped you draw this inference?

_____

_____

5. What can you infer about how Abby feels toward her brother?

_____

_____

6. What are three clues in the text that helped you draw this inference?

_____

_____

MAKING INFERENCES

Viktor's Room

Viktor's room is a mess and his dad won't let him go out until he cleans it. Viktor complains that it's his sister Sarah's fault.

"Sarah left her doll on the floor!" he yells.

"Besides that, whose games and books are on the floor?" his dad patiently replies.

"I don't know how those got there! The guys must have left it when they came over the other day."

Viktor's father isn't buying it. "What about your unmade bed?" he asks, trying to hide his smile. "Did the guys do that too?"

"Probably! They were wrestling, so they must have knocked the covers off!"

Viktor's father shakes his head and sighs. "You still have to clean it up before you go out."

Viktor stomps into his room. He mutters under his breath about his sister and his friends. Then he starts throwing books onto his bookshelf and slamming drawers. Suddenly the door opens and Sarah walks in.

"I'll help you, Viktor." She picks up her doll and starts to put the games away. Viktor watches her for a minute. He remembers how he blamed his room on her, and she's just a little kid.

"Thanks," he says. "I'll take you out for ice cream after we clean up, okay?"

MAKING INFERENCES

For every inference you make, give three clues from the text.

1. What can you infer about Viktor's character traits? _____

_____

_____

2. What are three clues in the text that helped you draw this inference?

_____

_____

3. What can you infer about how Viktor's father is feeling?

_____

_____

4. What are three clues in the text that helped you draw this inference?

_____

_____

5. What can you infer about how Viktor feels at the end of the story?

_____

_____

6. What are three clues in the text that helped you draw this inference?

_____

_____

UNDERSTANDING SETTING

Remember: The *setting* is where a story takes place. A story can have one setting or many settings.

Read the passage. Then answer the questions.

It all started with brussels sprouts.

Tonight is my first night at Mob Middle School, which has me kind of creeped out. It's a time when a guy could really use a pork chop—burned to a crisp, just how I like it. But instead, Mom served me brussels sprouts!

See, she's all into this new cookbook: *30 Days to a Greener You*. Dad tells her, "Honey, you're as green as the day I met you." But that just makes her all weepy-eyed. Then they end up kissing or something. (GROSS!)

So let me say that I am not a fan of this green diet. Creepers don't eat brussels sprouts. It's not normal!

...I would have fed them to my pet dog, except I don't have one. I have a pet squid named Sticky.

And if I tried to feed them to Sticky, Mom would notice the gross green hunks floating in the aquarium. So I tried to feed them to my baby sister when Mom wasn't looking. But Cammy just threw them across the floor like bouncy balls.

When Dad scolded her, she scrunched up her face and did what she always does. She blew up. Yup, right there at the kitchen table. I almost wished I'd died in the blast and respawned somewhere else—like in a normal family's kitchen.

*From <u>The Creeper Diaries: Mob School Survivor</u> by Greyson Mann,   Sky Pony Press, 2017.

UNDERSTANDING SETTING

1. Write your answers to the questions below.

    A. What is the setting for the story?

    _____

    _____

    B. Give two clues that tell you where the setting is.

    _____

    _____

    C. Do you think this story might have another setting later on?
       If so, where might it be?

    _____

    _____

    D. What is the clue that tells you where a second setting might be?

    _____

    _____

2. Underline the words below that could be a setting for a story.

a dentist's office	a friend	reading a book
a bike store	a playground	playing
the Overworld	your teacher	your bedroom

CHARACTERS

Read the passage. Then answer the questions.

Well, the night started out okay. When Sam and his dad came to pick me up, my family wasn't TOO embarrassing. Except the Fashion Queen came downstairs wearing some stinky new gunpowder perfume.

I told Sam that my sister, Cate (a.k.a. the Fashion Queen) was trying to impress some guy named Steve. Sam laughed and said that her plan might not work, because Cate smelled like rotten eggs.

I don't really think Sam is one to talk, after that spoiled milk spilled all over him at school. But I let it slide. I've been doing that a lot with him lately.

Things were going pretty much okay until we got to Sam's house near the swamp. That's when three mini slimes bounced out of the house to greet us. Sam patted them all on their little slime heads.

TRIPLETS? As much as Sam talks, you'd think he might have mentioned that he has three little brothers.

Let's just say that I'm not a fan of little kids. They're loud and germy. Those mini Sams were oozing slime EVERYWHERE. I didn't want to touch anything!

But things got worse when we went inside the house. I smelled it before I saw it—a CAT. Here's what you should know about me and cats: we don't get along. Not at all.

Adapted from <u>The Creeper Diaries: Mob School Survivor</u> by Greyson Mann, Sky Pony Press, 2017.

CHARACTER TRAITS

Remember: Character *traits* are the parts of a person's personality. Readers get clues about a character's traits by how the person acts, thinks, and talks. A character trait is not an emotion or a feeling; feelings come and go, but traits are part of who a person is.

Reread the passage on the previous page. Then fill out the chart based on what you know about these three characters.

Character	Traits	Evidence
narrator		
Sam		
"Fashion Queen" Cate		

CONFLICT

> **Remember:** In a story, the *conflict* is an event, a person (or people), or a situation that stands in the way of a character's achieving his or her goal. The conflict forces the character to take action in some way.

Read the passage below, and then answer the questions.

Warren rushed over to Lily. "What's going on?"

"The zombies keep spawning," Lily cried.

The sky was growing dark. Warren suggested, "You can stay at my house. We can't be out here now. It's too dangerous."

It was too late. An army of zombies marched through town, striking any villager who was in their path. The vacant-eyed mob ripped doors from their hinges, forcing the villagers to flee from their homes.

Lily checked her inventory. She had enough potions and arrows. Lily sprinted toward the zombie army with her diamond sword and slammed it against as many zombies as she could hit. Warren splashed potions on the zombies, weakening them. He aimed his bow and arrow and shot arrows into the mob. A villager fought alongside Warren and Lily, but she was hit by a fireball and destroyed. They were outnumbered.

"What are we going to do?" Lily cried. She was starting to panic. If she didn't destroy this mob of zombies, she would never make it back home again. She desperately wanted her family—her mom and dad, her cat, even her younger brother. If only she and Warren could find a way to defeat the mob and keep them from spawning.

Adapted from Mobs in the Mine: An Unofficial Minetrapped Adventure, Book 2, by Winter Morgan, Sky Pony Press, 2016.

CONFLICT

Reread the passage on the previous page. Then answer the questions that follow.

1. What is the main conflict in the story?

   _____

   _____

2. What is the conflict preventing the character from achieving?

   _____

   _____

3. What type of conflict does the story show?
   Circle the correct answer.

   A. Conflict between the hero and nature
   B. Conflict between the hero and herself
   C. Conflict between the hero and others

4. Another type of conflict that could come out later in this story might be:

   A. Conflict between Lily and Warren
   B. Conflict between Lily and a terrible thunderstorm
   C. Conflict between Lily and her own fear
   D. All of the above

PLOT STRUCTURE

Remember A *plot* starts with an introduction, then has rising action, reaches a climax, has falling action, and finally comes to a resolution.

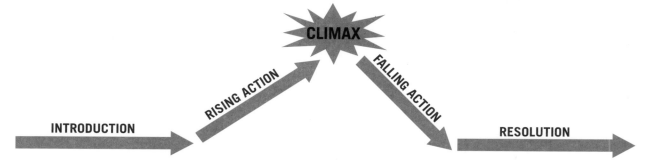

Read the passage below, and then answer the questions.

Mud flew this way and that as Will dug madly into the earth. He knew that thunderstorms were bad news. Not only would monsters spawn, but they could be super charged by lightning. He had to finish his shelter right now.

He heard the moans of two zombies before he saw them. Two—no, three—staggered across the ground, arms outstretched. Will pulled out his bow and launched arrows, one after another. The first zombie dropped with a grunt.

Will's heart pounded as he turned back toward his shelter. Zombies are slow, he told himself. I can make it—I can finish this in time. He dug out a few more blocks of dirt. Then he grabbed his bow and arrow and whirled around again.

Yikes! The two zombies were just a few feet away. Will dropped his bow and grabbed his sword instead. He stepped forward, swinging the sword. With a few strong strokes, he took down the first monster. The iron sword was amazing!

With a surge of confidence, Will attacked the second zombie. The monster growled and groaned before falling backward, dropping chunks of rotten flesh.

Will pumped his sword toward the sky. "Yeah!" he shouted. "Take that, you dirty mobs!"

Will turned and ran back. He was able to finish his shelter before any other mobs attacked.

Adapted from Lost in the Jungle: Secrets of an Overworld Survivor, Book 1 by Greyson Mann, Sky Pony Press, 2017.

CONFLICT

Reread the passage on the previous page and then answer the questions.

1. Describe the introduction in the passage.

_____

_____

_____

2. What is the rising action in the passage?

_____

_____

_____

3. What is the passage's climax?

_____

_____

4. Describe the falling action in the passage.

_____

_____

_____

5. Explain the resolution in the passage.

_____

_____

_____

COMPARING FACTS FROM TWO TEXTS

Read the passages below, and then answer the questions on the next page.

Text 1: Shulkers

The shulkers are hostile mobs found in the End city. They often lurk at the entrance, inside the towers, and protecting chests. The name shulker is short for "shell lurker." These mobs hide in a one-block, cubed, armored purple shell that looks very much like an ordinary purpur block. They generally don't move and attach themselves to solid blocks. They are well hidden against the purpur walls and floors of the End cities, where they spawn. Every so often the shell opens, and inside you can see a small face. When a target comes within sixteen blocks of this creature, it will open up and shoot bullets.

Text 2: Endermen

Endermen are three-block-tall black mobs with very long arms and legs. They wander about the Overworld and the End in their own little clouds of purple stars. They occasionally pick up a block and hold it. Endermen are neutral unless you provoke them, which happens by simply looking at them anywhere from their upper legs to their head. When provoked, they open their mouths and shake with rage. Endermen spawn on solid blocks at light level 7 or less. They often spawn in the End in packs of four.

COMPARING FACTS FROM TWO TEXTS

Fill out the worksheet based on the two texts you read.

Text 1: Facts

Text 2: Facts

_____   _____

_____   _____

_____   _____

_____   _____

_____   _____

_____   _____

_____   _____

How are the facts alike and different?

_____

_____

_____

_____

_____

_____

_____

_____

INTERPRETING CHARTS

Read the passage and charts. Then answer the questions.

Swords and axes are great weapons to keep in your inventory. The greater the attack speed (measured in swings per second), the faster the speed of the weapon and the less time it takes to recharge. The greater the attack damage, the more damage the weapon will inflict.

TYPES OF SWORDS	ATTACK SPEED	ATTACK DAMAGE
Diamond Sword	1.6	7
Gold Sword	1.6	4
Iron Sword	1.6	6
Stone Sword	1.6	5
Wooden Sword	1.6	4

TYPES OF AXES	ATTACK SPEED	ATTACK DAMAGE
Diamond Axe	1	9
Gold Axe	.9	9
Iron Axe	.8	9
Stone Axe	1	7
Wooden Axe	.8	7

*From *Mini Hacks for Minecrafters: Mastering 1.9* by Megan Miller, Sky Pony Press, 2016.

INTEGRATING KNOWLEDGE FROM TEXTS

Answer the questions.

1. What is the attack speed of every sword?

_____

2. Which swords have the greatest attack damage?

_____

3. Which swords have the least attack damage?

_____

4. Which axes have the slowest attack speed?

_____

5. Which axes have the greatest attack speed?

_____

6. Which axes have the greatest attack damage?

_____

7. Which axes have the least attack damage?

_____

8. Overall, which type of weapon (sword or axe) has greater

attack speed? _____

9. Overall, which type of weapon (sword or axe) has greater attack

damage? _____

READING FLUENCY

Read the following passage out loud to practice your reading fluency. Use the chart on the next page to record how many words you can read correctly in a minute! Reread the passage every few days to track your progress.

Cave Spiders

To defeat the cave spider, you need to kill existing and spawning spiders and disable or destroy the spawner itself. Because they are so fast, you will be using a sword against them instead of the bow. This is because the bow takes several moments to pull and charge before you can fire an arrow.

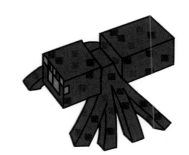

You will find yourself trying to battle these spiders at the same time as trying to destroy enough cobwebs around the spawner so that you can disable it. You can use a bucket of water to remove cobwebs, and shears are the fastest tool to cut them. Water will also uproot any torches placed on the ground, so be aware of where your torches are.

One tactic is to close off the ends of the area where you know there's a spawner, and then tunnel in just above or below the spawner. Then you can quickly destroy it with your pickaxe or place torches on either side. Placing torches will create enough light that it prevents spiders from spawning.

Try to avoid letting these spiders get above you, where they can jump on you and damage you. The venom from their bite will cause you enough damage to bring you down to a half-heart of health. It won't kill you, but it will leave you very weak. Once you are bitten, retreat and use potions or milk to heal before you strike again. If you don't care about losing the spawner or any drops and experience points, you can pour a bucket of lava on it.

Adapted from Hacks for Minecrafters: Combat Edition by Megan Miller, Sky Pony Press, 2014.

READING FLUENCY CHART

Have an adult help you chart your reading fluency.

1. Set a timer for one minute and start reading until the minute is up. Mark your stopping point on the passage. (Fast readers can count the words they read in 30 seconds and multiply that number by two.)

2. A friend or adult records the "words wrong" info on the chart below as you read.

3. Subtract the number of words you got wrong from the total number of words you read. This is called the "Words Correct Per Minute" (WCPM) number.

Date	Number of Words Read in 1 Minute	Number of Words Wrong	WCPM

Words I Missed:

READING FLUENCY

Read the following passage to practice your reading fluency. Use the chart on the next page to record how many words you can read correctly in a minute! Reread the passage every few days to track your progress.

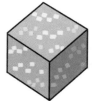

The Ice Biome

"Let's get going," said Jack. "We want to get to the cold biome before dark."

"Maybe we can build an igloo once we're there," suggested Toby.

The group trekked toward the cold biome and walked up a large mountain. Harriet paused at the top of the mountain. "I wonder if we could spot William's town from up here."

Jack searched the landscape, looking for signs of life. "I feel just like William and Oliver. It is beautiful up here."

Toby stared at the icy biome that was on the other side of the mountain. "I can't wait to slide on the ice. It looks like so much fun. And I want to have a snowball fight."

"We don't have time for silly games," scolded Harriet. "We're here to find William."

The gang made their way down the steep mountain toward the ice biome. They passed an unusually tall patch of snow and Harriet was the first to go over to check it out.

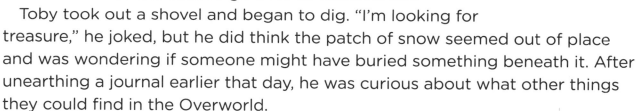

Toby took out a shovel and began to dig. "I'm looking for treasure," he joked, but he did think the patch of snow seemed out of place and was wondering if someone might have buried something beneath it. After unearthing a journal earlier that day, he was curious about what other things they could find in the Overworld.

Harriet joined Toby. "Let's place a hopper here for the snow to collect in." She set one up right next to them. Jack started digging too.

"I see something!" Angela shouted to the others.

"What is it?" asked Jack.

"I think it's a chest," said Toby.

"Open it!" Jack and Harriet stood next to him, waiting.

Toby opened the chest. "Blue helmets! It's filled with blue helmets!"

From Discoveries in the Overworld: Lost Minecraft Journals, Book 1 by Winter Morgan, Sky Pony Press, 2015.

READING FLUENCY CHART

Have an adult help you chart your reading fluency.

1. Set a timer for one minute and start reading until the minute is up. Mark your stopping point on the passage. (Fast readers can count the words they read in 30 seconds and multiply that number by two.)

2. A friend or adult records the "words wrong" info on the chart below as you read.

3. Subtract the number of words you got wrong from the total number of words you read. This is called the "Words Correct Per Minute" (WCPM) number.

Date	Number of Words Read in 1 Minute	Number of Words Wrong	WCPM

Words I Missed:

READING FLUENCY

Read the following passage to practice your reading fluency. Use the chart on the next page to record how many words you can read correctly in a minute! Reread the passage every few days to track your progress.

The Attack of Mr. Anarchy

Lily grabbed the potion of Harming from her inventory and doused Mr. Anarchy.

"Attack him!" she called out to the others.

Michael and Simon stormed over to Mr. Anarchy, striking the sinister villain with their diamond swords.

"Stop!" Mr. Anarchy called out. "I'll tell you what you want to know."

They didn't listen to Mr. Anarchy. They struck him with their swords, just as two skeletons spawned in the small prison cell.

"Oh no!" Mr. Anarchy yelled. A skeleton shot an arrow at Mr. Anarchy.

"We have to get out of here!" Lily called to her friends.

The group darted from the prison. They scurried down the hall of the jungle temple, dodging arrows from the blue griefers that monitored the hall.

"Faster!" Lily cried to the group.

They ran as fast as they could until they exited the jungle temple. Lily hid behind a large patch of leaves. The others joined her. They grabbed their bows and arrows from their inventories and shot arrows at the blue griefers.

Then Michael spotted someone running past the soldiers.

"Do you see that person?" he asked the others.

"Yes," Simon responded, taking a second look at the person. "Mr. Anarchy must have respawned. We have to get out of here!"

Just then, skeletons and zombies spawned in the jungle temple, as magma cubes bounced toward the blue griefers. The gang hid behind the bark of a large tree and watched the blue griefers struggle to defeat the undead mobs and the cubes from the Nether.

Text adapted from <u>Mobs in the Mine: An Unofficial Minetrapped Adventure</u> by Winter Morgan, Sky Pony Press, 2015

READING FLUENCY CHART

Have an adult help you chart your reading fluency.

1. Set a timer for one minute and start reading until the minute is up. Mark your stopping point on the passage. (Fast readers can count the words they read in 30 seconds and multiply that number by two.)

2. A friend or adult records the "words wrong" info on the chart below as you read.

3. Subtract the number of words you got wrong from the total number of words you read. This is called the "Words Correct Per Minute" (WCPM) number.

Date	Number of Words Read in 1 Minute	Number of Words Wrong	WCPM

Words I Missed:

READING FLUENCY

Read the following passage to practice your reading fluency. Use the chart on the next page to record how many words you can read correctly in a minute! Reread the passage every few days to track your progress.

Minecrafting Enchantments

Enchanting and brewing potions can be challenging for beginners. Usually these activities will have to wait until you've gathered the proper resources. However, getting to this point should be a major goal if you want to survive well in Normal or Hard mode. Enchanted weapons and armor make a huge difference in surviving combat. They are absolutely necessary for fighting the strongest mobs, like the Ender Dragon and Wither.

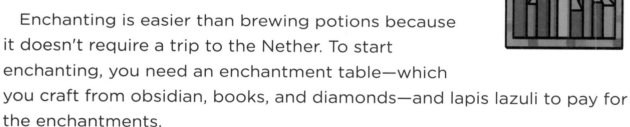

Enchanting is easier than brewing potions because it doesn't require a trip to the Nether. To start enchanting, you need an enchantment table—which you craft from obsidian, books, and diamonds—and lapis lazuli to pay for the enchantments.

There are different levels for enchantments. For example, a Protection IV enchantment will give more protection than a Protection I enchantment. The level of enchantment you can give to an item is increased by surrounding the table with up to fifteen bookshelves.

To enchant, click on the enchantment table and place the item you want to enchant in the left slot. In the right panel, you'll be given three choices of enchantment. It will tell you how many experience levels you need to perform the enchantment, as well as how many lapis lazuli (and how many experience levels) it will cost.

Select the enchantment you want on the right and then remove your enchanted item. Sometimes you will get extra enchantments with the one you picked. Enchanted items have a magical glow.

Text adapted from Hacks for Minecrafters: Combat Edition by Megan Miller, Sky Pony Press, 2014

READING FLUENCY CHART

Have an adult help you chart your reading fluency.

1. Set a timer for one minute and start reading until the minute is up. Mark your stopping point on the passage. (Fast readers can count the words they read in 30 seconds and multiply that number by two.)

2. A friend or adult records the "words wrong" info on the chart below as you read.

3. Subtract the number of words you got wrong from the total number of words you read. This is called the "Words Correct Per Minute" (WCPM) number.

Date	Number of Words Read in 1 Minute	Number of Words Wrong	WCPM

Words I Missed:

ANSWER KEY

PAGE 2

1. unpack

defuse

reread

undertake

overdo

outlive

2. reopen

undo

deactivate

outran

PAGE 3

1. loud

louder

loudest

funny

funnier

funniest

2. er

harder

est

happier

iest

longest

PAGE 4

A. dis

B. mis

C. co

D. ir

E. dis

F. dis

2. Answers may vary. Some answers include:

discover

irrational

reappear

mistrust

displace

PAGE 5

A. less

B. ness

C. ment

D. less

E. ment

F. ness

2. Answers may vary. Some answers include:

hopeful

basement

enjoyment

careless

darkness

sadness

PAGE 6

chase   smelt   make   brew

teleport   slime   cake   cast

blaze   plank   steep   tame

2. Answers may vary.

PAGE 7

1. A. cutting

B. digging

C. fanning

D. bedding

E. stopping

F. planning

G. stunning

H. tripping

2.

ORIGINAL WORD	-ing	Final word
win	-ing	winning
map	-ing	mapping
get	-ing	getting
wag	a-ing	wagging

PAGE 8

1. A. boxes

B. kisses

C. matches

D. bushes

E. mixes

F. witches

G. crashes

H. lunches

PAGE 8 (CONTINUED)

2. Fill out the chart, writing the original word before the plural -es was added.

ORIGINAL WORD	-es	Final word
sandwich	-es	sandwiches
wish	-es	wishes
catch	-es	catches
hoax	-es	hoaxes

PAGE 9

1. The kids are playing in **their** school's playground. In a few minutes, **they're** going to play a game of tag. The school is over **there**.

2. Cassie drew **two** clouds.
Enrico wants **to** go home soon.
"I want to play **too**," said James.

3. A. "What are you drawing over **here**?" Dennis asked. [here / hear]

　B. "What? I didn't **hear** you," Cassie said. [here / hear]

　C. "Is that **your** basketball?" Penny asked. [your / you're]

　D. "**You're** going to be late getting home," Enrico warned. [your / you're]

PAGE 10

1. A. Turn into　　　**transform**
　B. Destroy　　　**obliterate**
　C. Get away from　**elude**
　D. Speed up　　　**expedite**
　E. Call, gather　　**summon**

2. A. Warn, signal　　**alert**
　B. Harm, strike　　**attack**
　C. Foes, rivals　　**enemies**

PAGE 11

3. A. Make better　　**obliterate**
　B. Keep the same　**transform**
　C. Send away　　　**summon**
　D. Catch, tackle　　**elude**
　E. Slow down　　　**expedite**

4. A. Capture, find　　**escape**
　B. Distant, far away **nearby**
　C. Quick, speedy　　**slow**

PAGE 12

1.
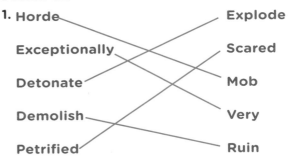

Horde — Mob
Exceptionally — Very
Detonate — Explode
Demolish — Ruin
Petrified — Scared

2. A. **blast**　　Explosion, boom
　B. **protect**　Defend, shield
　C. **hidden**　Concealed, unseen

PAGE 13

3. Horde　　　　few
Exceptionally　slightly
Detonate　　　implode
Demolish　　　fix
Petrified　　　fearless

4. A. **easy**　　　Hard, difficult
　B. **quiet**　　Loud, noisy
　C. **dark**　　　Bright, sunny

PAGE 14

1. Appears　　　**arrives**
Charging　　　**rushing**
Activates　　　**triggers**
Spawns　　　　**reproduces**
Glowing　　　　**shining**

2. A. Doorway, entry　**portal**
　B. Dives, plunges　**swoops**
　C. Destroys, exterminates　**kills**

PAGE 15

3.
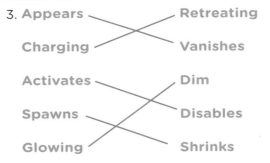

Appears — Vanishes
Charging — Retreating
Activates — Disables
Spawns — Shrinks
Glowing — Dim

58

4. A. Upper, topmost   <u>lower</u>
   B. Swallows, sips   <u>spits</u>
   C. Picks up   <u>drops</u>

PAGE 16

1. <u>sustenance</u>   food
2. <u>assemble</u>   to make or put something together
3. <u>lumber</u>   a piece of wood
4. <u>inventory</u>   a collection of supplies

PAGE 17

1. Require   c
   Provide   b
   Till   a
   Distribute   a
   Excavate   b
   Impart   b
   Deter   a

2. A. <u>flat</u>
   B. <u>moves</u>
   C. <u>eating</u>

PAGE 18

1. <u>durable</u>   very strong
2. <u>damage</u>   harm, injury
3. <u>starvation</u>   having no food to eat
4. <u>suffocation</u>   having no air to breathe

PAGE 19

Word	Definition
craft	make, create
shield	protect, defend
enchanted	given a charm
glint	shine, sparkle
mine	dig up
armor	protective covering
explosion	blast, burst

2. A. Chestplate: **A piece of armor that protects the chest.**
   B. Common: **Ordinary, found everywhere**

PAGE 20

Note: Answers may vary. This is a sample of possible answers.
1. What is the main idea of this text?
The main idea of the text is that an igloo makes a good pit stop if you are in a snowy biome and get cold or hungry.
2. List three details that support the main idea.
A. Igloos have everything you need.
B. Igloos have food stored on shelves.
C. Igloos have blankets and warm clothes.

PAGE 21

1. C
2. A
3. A
4. B

PAGE 22–23

Note: Answers may vary. This is a sample of possible answers.
Compare
  Skeletons and zombies travel in mobs.
  Skeletons and zombies burn in sunlight.
  Skeletons and zombies cannot see through glass.

Contrast
  Skeletons drop bones and arrows; zombies drop rotten flesh, carrots, and potatoes.
  Skeletons are hard to defeat; zombies are easy to defeat.
  Skeletons spawn alone; zombies spawn in groups of four.

PAGE 24

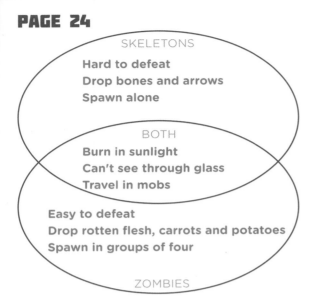

SKELETONS

Hard to defeat
Drop bones and arrows
Spawn alone

BOTH

Burn in sunlight
Can't see through glass
Travel in mobs

Easy to defeat
Drop rotten flesh, carrots and potatoes
Spawn in groups of four

ZOMBIES

PAGE 25

Ingredient	Icon
Glistering melon	**Watermelon**
Pufferfish	Pufferfish
Spider eye	**Red spider eye**
Sugar	Sugar crystal
Golden carrot	**Yellow carrot**
Ghast tear	**Teardrop**
Blaze powder	Fire

PAGE 26

E   Glistering melon

F   Pufferfish

D   Spider eye

A   Sugar

B   Golden carrot

G   Ghast tear

C   Blaze powder

PAGES 27–28

7   Will hopes he doesn't catch a pufferfish.

2   Mina teases Will.

5   Will gives Mina the fish.

3   Will blames Mina for his bad luck.

4   Mina holds out her hand for the fish.

9   Will unhooks the salmon.

6   Will casts his fishing line.

8   Will reels in a salmon.

10 Will feels uneasy.

1   Will reels in a pufferfish.

PAGES 29–30

5   Will puts the saddle on the pig.

2   Will digs up a carrot.

1   Will grabs his fishing pole.

3   Will puts the carrot on the fishhook.

6   Will gets into the saddle.

8   The pig begins to trot.

4   Will hurries back to the pigpen.

7   Will holds the carrot in front of the pig's nose.

PAGE 31

"I need a sword!" Lucy cried out, looking frantically at the skeletons.

Eric crouched on the ground in the forest. The sun had set a long time ago, and it was hard to see. He felt through his inventory and found his spare sword. It wasn't ideal, but at least he could give something to Lucy. He hoped it would do. He handed it to Lucy.

"I'm sorry, but I only have a wooden sword."

"That's better than nothing! Thanks!"

Eric started to battle the skeletons with his powerful diamond sword, which he always fought with. He sprinted toward the two skeletons that Lucy had cornered. With a blow from his diamond sword, he defeated one of them. Lucy battled the other one with her wooden sword until it was destroyed.

"We make a great team," Eric said with a smile.

"The fight's not over yet," Lucy said as six new skeletons suddenly appeared and shot arrows at them. Eric's response was cut off as an arrow pierced his leg.

Lucy ran over to her friend and splashed a potion of Invisibility on him. Now the skeletons wouldn't be able to shoot more arrows at Eric.

"We need to find the spawner before it makes more skeletons. Let's go!"

PAGE 32

1. Who are the main characters in the story?
   Lucy and Eric are the main characters in the story.
2. What are the main characters battling?
   The characters are battling skeletons.
3. What time of day does this story take place?
   The story takes place at night.
4. Where does the arrow pierce Eric?
   The arrow pierces Eric in the leg.
5. Why does Lucy say, "The fight's not over yet"?
   Lucy says, "The fight's not over yet" because six more skeletons appeared.
6. How are the skeletons multiplying?
   The skeletons are multiplying from a spawner.

PAGES 33–34

Note: Answers may vary. This is a sample of possible answers.

What can you infer about Abby's character traits?
Abby is a neat and careful person. She is creative and kind.

What are three clues in the text that helped you draw this inference?
She shows she is careful by putting everything away neatly.
She shows she is creative by having a workshop and making projects.
She shows she is kind by looking out for her dog and her brother's safety.

What can you infer about the types of projects Abby makes?
Abby makes things out of wood.

What are three clues in the text that helped you draw this inference?
She has tools such as a saw, hammer, and pliers.
She keeps nails and screws in a box on her desk.
She sweeps up sawdust at the end of the day.

What can you infer about how Abby feels toward her brother?
Abby cares about her brother and wants to teach him how to make things when he is older.

What are three clues in the text that helped you draw this inference?
She tucks in her stool so her baby brother won't trip over it.
She likes to take her brother into her workshop and show him things.
She hopes he'll want to make things with her when he is older.

PAGES 35–36

Note: Answers may vary. This is a sample of possible answers.

What can you infer about Viktor's character traits?
Viktor is messy, blames other people for his mistakes, and gets angry easily.

What are three clues in the text that helped you draw this inference?
Viktor's room is a mess.
Viktor blames his friends and his sister for the way his room is.
Viktor stomps into his room and throws things around.

What can you infer about how Viktor's father is feeling?
Viktor's father is trying to be patient and reason with his son.

What are three clues in the text that helped you draw this inference?
He talks patiently to Viktor.
He points out that his friends probably didn't make the whole mess.
He shakes his head and sighs but says Viktor still has to clean his room.

PAGES 35–36 (CONTINUED)

What can you infer about how Viktor feels at the end of the story?
Viktor feels guilty when his sister comes to help him clean.

What are three clues in the text that helped you draw this inference?
Viktor realizes he blamed her for his mess.
Viktor knows she is just a little kid and doesn't deserve his blame.
Viktor says he will take her out for ice cream.

PAGES 37–38

1. What is the setting for the story?
The setting is the dinner table in the home of the narrator.

Give two clues that tell you where the setting is.
A. The family is having dinner.
B. The baby sister cries at the kitchen table.

Do you think this story might have another setting later on? If so, where might it be?
Yes, I think the story will have a second setting at Mob Middle School.

What is the clue that tells you where a second setting might be?
The narrator says, "Tonight is my first night at Mob Middle School."

2. a dentist's office, a bike store, the Overworld, a friend, a playground, your teacher, reading a book, playing, your bedroom

PAGES 39–40

Note: Answers may vary. This is a sample of possible answers.

Character	Traits	Evidence
narrator	Grouchy	Doesn't like little kids, doesn't like cats, doesn't expect the night to go well
Sam	Good-natured Talkative	Jokes about rotten egg smell. Narrator says he talks a lot.
"Fashion Queen" Cate	Dramatic Cares about appearances	Likes attention, trying to impress Steve nickname is "Fashion Queen"

PAGES 41–42

1. What is the main conflict in the story?
The main conflict is a battle between Lily and Warren and a mob of zombies.

2. What is the conflict preventing the character from achieving?
The conflict is preventing Lily from going home.

3. What type of conflict does the story show?
C. Conflict between the hero and others

4. Another type of conflict that could come out later in this story might be:
D. All of the above

PAGE 43–44

1. Describe the introduction in the passage.
   The story starts with Will digging a shelter.
2. What is the rising action in the passage?
   The rising action starts when we learn that Will has to dig the shelter quickly because of the approaching thunderstorm and the zombies. Then the rising action continues with the zombies attacking and Will fighting them off.
3. What is the passage's climax?
   The climax is when Will destroys the last zombie.
4. Describe the falling action in the passage.
   The falling action starts when the last zombie groans and drops chunks of rotting flesh. The falling action continues with Will celebrating his victory.
5. Explain the resolution in the passage.
   The resolution is when Will is able to complete his shelter.

PAGES 45–46

Note: Answers may vary. This is a sample of possible answers.

Text 1: Facts
   Hostile mob
   Purple one-block cubes
   Blend in with their surroundings
   Generally don't move
   Spawn in End cities
   Shoots bullets at targets within 16 blocks

Text 2: Facts
   Neutral mob
   Three blocks tall, black, long arms and legs
   Do not blend in with surroundings
   Wander about the Overworld and the End
   Spawn in End cities
   Don't attack unless provoked

How the Facts Are Alike and Different
   Both shulkers and Endermen are mobs, but shulkers are hostile and Endermen are neutral. Shulkers are only one block tall, while Endermen are three blocks tall. Shulkers hide in purple armor and blend in with their surroundings of purpur blocks. Endermen are very noticeable: they are black with long arms and legs. Shulkers generally don't move, while Endermen wander about the Overworld. Both shulkers and Endermen spawn in the End. Shulkers will shoot bullets at a target that comes within sixteen blocks. Endermen do not attack, unless they are provoked by looking at them above their legs. Then, they open their mouths and shake with rage.

PAGES 47–48

1. What is the attack speed of every sword?
   They all have the an attack speed of 1.6.
2. Which swords have the greatest attack damage?
   The diamond sword has the greatest attack damage.
3. Which swords have the least attack damage?
   The gold sword and the wooden sword have the least attack damage.
4. Which axes have the slowest attack speed?
   The iron axe and the wooden axe have the slowest attack speed.
5. Which axes have the greatest attack speed?
   The diamond axe and the stone axe have the greatest attack speed.
6. Which axes have the greatest attack damage?
   The diamond, gold, and iron axes have the greatest attack damage.
7. Which axes have the least attack damage?
   The stone axe and the wooden axe have the least attack damage.
8. Overall, which type of weapon (sword or axe) has greater attack speed?
   The sword has greater attack speed.
9. Overall, which type of weapon (sword or axe) has greater attack damage?
   The axe has greater attack damage.